Sonny Thoughts For Cloudy Days

From the Heart and Soul

Of

Sonny Grosso

This book is dedicated to Bella. Truly an Angel walking on Earth. Her encouragement and belief in me and my "Thoughts" keep me thinking every day!

To all my Facebook friends who supported me on a daily basis.

To My Mom and Dad who taught me a way of looking at life that came to life in this book.

Anyone at any time is going through a struggle. We are not alone in this world. The key is not to dwell on darkness. Not to worry about what we "don't" have or miss and concentrate and be thankful for what we have. Each chapter of our life only brings us to the next. We can go back and review, read over etc. but not to linger in the past except to smile, remember and learn.

Learn from the innocence of a child. They are brave enough to dream out loud, speak from their heart, give unconditional love and look to the future with hope! Strive to find the child inside every day!

Fate is not the answer. God brings people together, what happens from there is up to them!

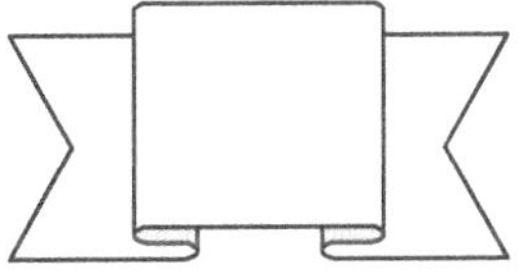

True love is "Sacred" when on solid ground. But shake it up and it becomes "Scared"! Stability will keep it alive and at peace!

The heart knows many things that the brain will never understand. Always listen to your heart!

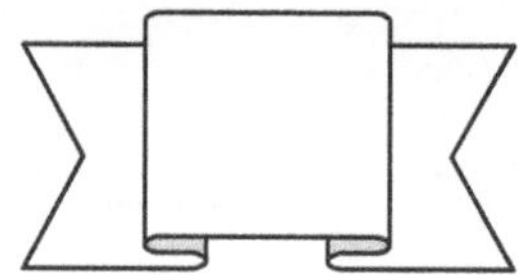

A person truly in love does not cry over the one they've lost. They cry FOR the one who has lost THEM!

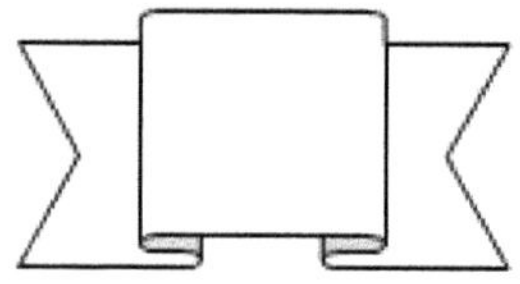

Fear and Insecurity are the mortal enemies of love and friendship!

Love will come and hold your hand for a while.
True love will come and hold your heart forever!

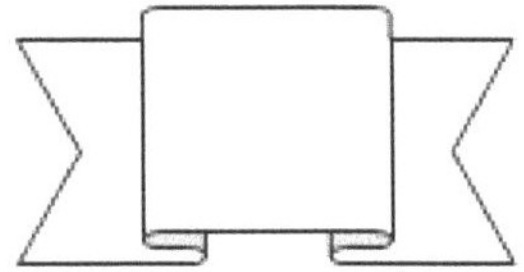

In any relationship, the three most important words besides "I Love You" are "I Am Sorry"!

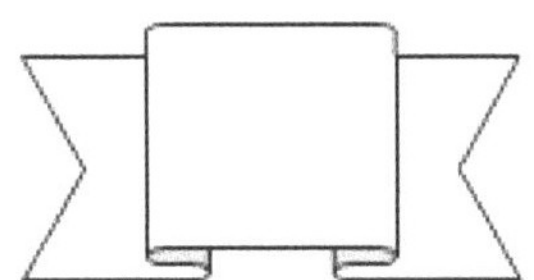

In any relationship, you are never as "perfect" as you are told you are in the beginning and never as "imperfect" as you are told you are in the end. Through it all, be yourself, like yourself, hold your head up high but your nose at a respectable level!

Belief and Hope are the glues that God's Angels use to mend a broken heart!

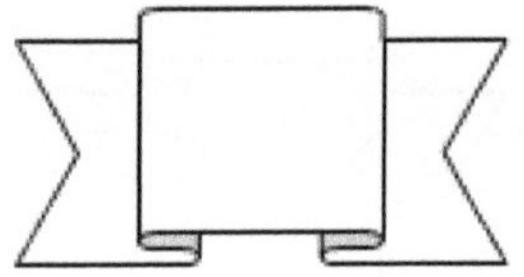

Angels walk amongst us every day. Look hard in the mirror, you just may be one and don't know it yet!

You have indeed found true love when you have found the one you you want to live for and die for. When you ask God to take their pain and give it to you!

Sometimes the clearest way you can tell a child you love them is to say "NO". Be a parent first, then a leader and then a friend!

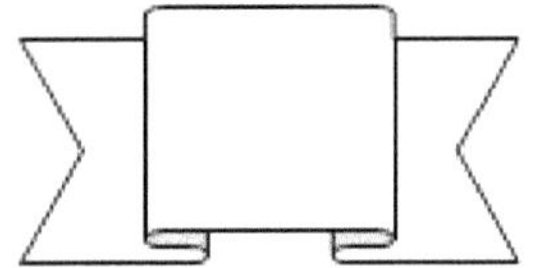

Always try your best to be a good, loving and caring person. But if you spend all your time trying to be a "perfect" person, you will find later on that you have wasted precious time!

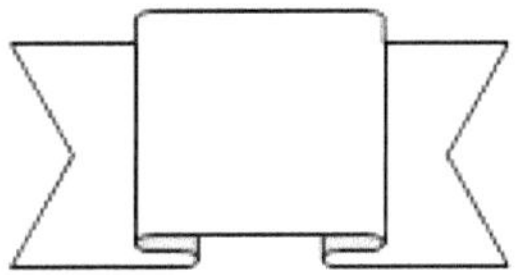

Be aware of the people who come in and out of your life only when it benefits them. Surround yourself with the ones who come into your life when it benefits YOU!

Try not to give your heart to someone you know is immature or seflish. They may not give it back as easily as they got it!

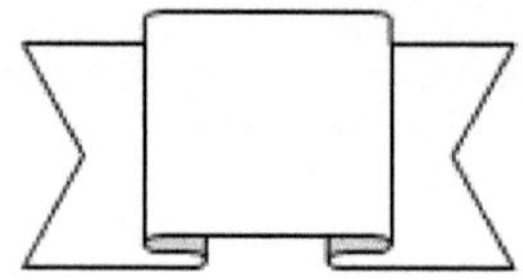

It is true that we never get a second chance to make a "first" impression. It is also true we never get a second chance to make a "last" one either. In between both, be the best person you can be!

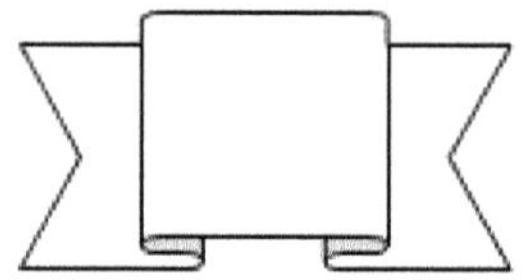

Sometimes when we are struggling, we are so happy to have people around us that we forget they all may not be there for support. Be careful who you choose to tell all your fears, secrets and desires to!

Every one of us has the ability to create a miracle. With a touch or a smile we can turn sorrow to joy. We can repair a broken heart, send a smile across the world and make dreams come true!

You can "close" your eyes and dream of love and happiness or "open" them and make your dreams come true!

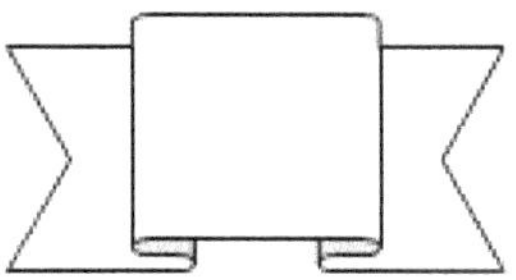

Don't spend so much time holding on to someone from YESTERDAY that you miss the chance to hold someone special TODAY and TOMORROW!

Whether you're riding in a Kia or a Benz, it's the people taking the ride with you that is important. Don't give up a Life of "love" for a Lifestyle of "things"!

There is a huge difference between being young at heart and acting your age!

Never hold your love or friendship hostage because it's not returned the same way. Offer it unconditionally from your heart. You are giving them a gift, the gift of YOU!

People judge us by the company we keep. God judges us by the way we treat that company. Give everyone you meet one of your smiles and hope they pass it on!

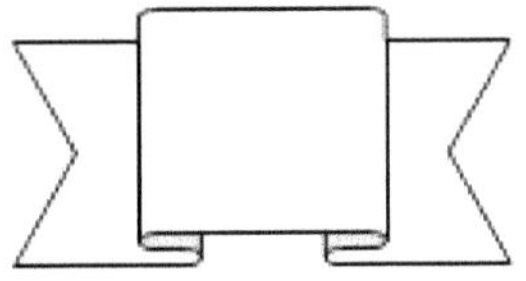

Don't mistake kindness for weakness, generosity for stupidity or love for dependency. Take the time to know the person while learning who **you** are at the same time!

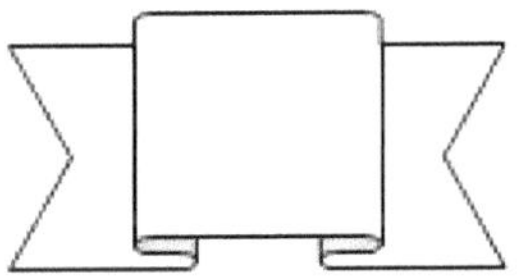

Some people live their lives in their own world. Never venturing out of their own circle of friends and family. That's fine but they should never assume that their way of life is the proper and ONLY way to live. We are all different, yet all the same!

Often times "indecision" is really "intuition". Always trust your instincts!

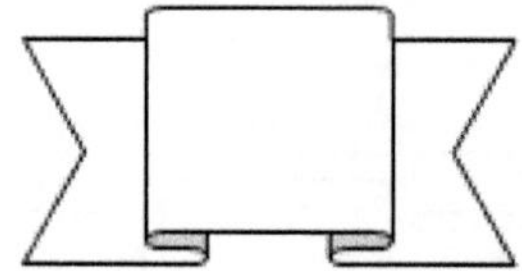

True love can be ellusive as a butterfly when being chased. But if you are alert and patient, it may come find you on its own!

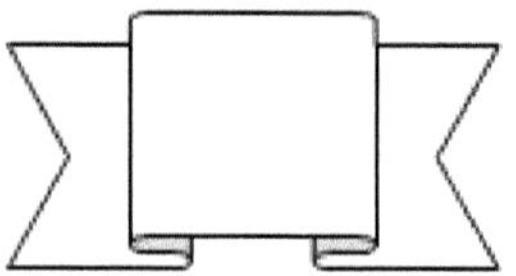

Don't waste precious time thinking about what you may be missing in life. Smile in contentment realizing that what "you" have, "others" may be missing!

Feelings of lonliness and despair do not come from a lack of love or affection. They come from a lack of confidence and direction. Know where you are going and believe you will get there!

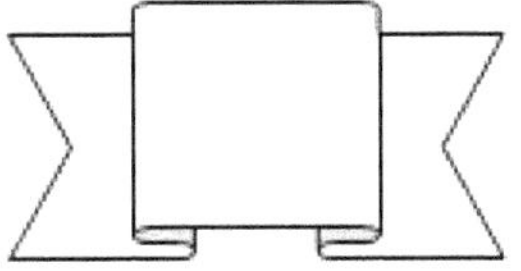

Love is not a game. A game has winners and losers.

When it's right, there are only winners!

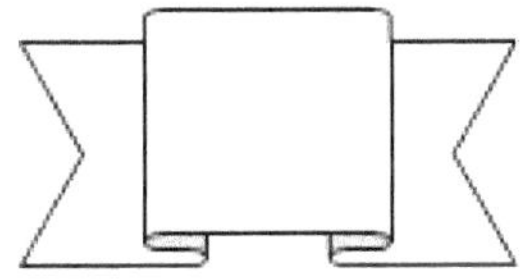

You can view your life as being stranded on an island surrounded by doubt and fear OR see your life on the same island surrounded by endless possibilities. It all depends on which view you choose!

Insecurity and Doubt can keep you awake all night. But Faith and Love can provide a wonderful bed and pillow to fall asleep on!

The "Highway of Life" has many exits and entrances. Fear and mistrust can force you to stay on the same road forever. Remember that if you take a wrong exit, there is another entrance ahead to get back on track. Drive on towards your dream, your love, your happiness!

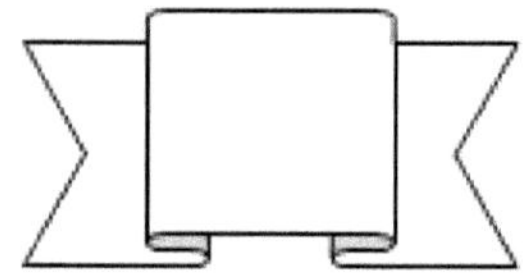

If you live your life going wherever the "wind" takes you, you may just "wind" up blown away!

Sometimes the "right" person is "right" in front of you but it's not the "right" time. Then you are "left" wondering if you "left" them for now, would there be anything "left" when you returned!

Whatever "IT" is, you can want it, dream of it or wish for it. But if you don't earn it, love it and respect it, you will eventually lose it and miss it!

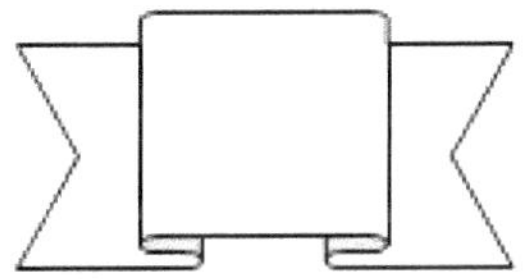

You can reach for the stars. Just make sure you aren't pushing the special people away with your outstretched arms. In the end, you may find that the real stars of your life were right there all along!

Just because someone has forgiven you, it doesn't mean it's an invitation back into their life. Forgiveness is the first step towards moving on or going back. Time will decide which!

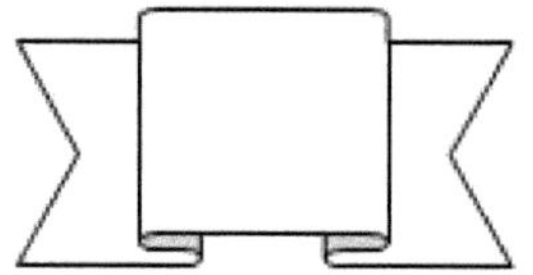

Being honest about a lie does not make you truthful! There are no half-truths or white lies in love and life!

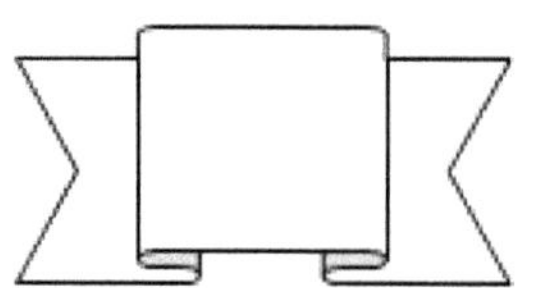

No relationship is 50/50. At any given moment, someone is giving more than the other. The key to its success is that it all BALANCES OUT in the long run. If both give 100%, oh the joys you will have!

Sometimes you can try so hard to change someone's opinion of you without success. Realize that it just may be THEY who need to change. Those who cannot see the good in you, will remain blind. Still be you!

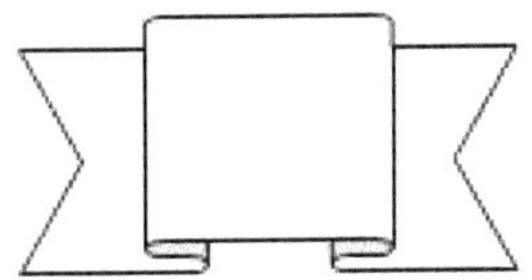

With the right person, you don't need heels to stand tall, muscles to show strength, lingerie to be sexy or jokes to make them smile!

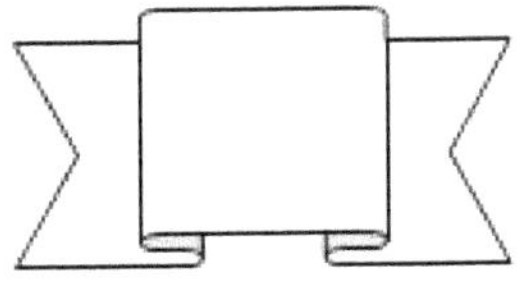

Mistakes and errors in judgement are God's way of showing us what we need to work on!

We were all born not knowing ANYTHING and will pass not knowing EVERYTHING. Be the best person you can in between!

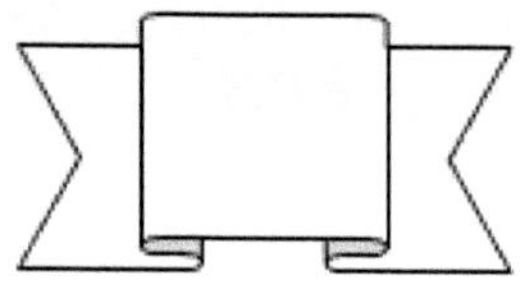

It's okay to blow up once in a while as long as you don't let it linger. But you must apologize when necssary and forgive yourself after!

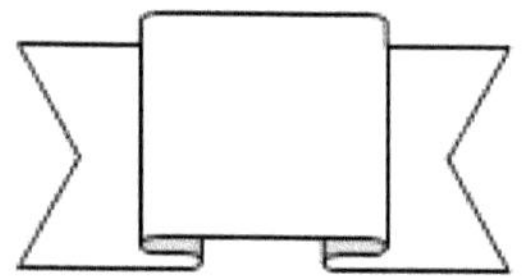

The biggest lie anyone can tell you or themselves is that they don't know what's right or wrong. Truth is they are struggling between doing what is right and what they want. Always do what's right!

The way to ease the pain of a broken heart is not to immediately move on to someone else. Take the time to heal, grieve, pray, examine the mistakes and accept it!

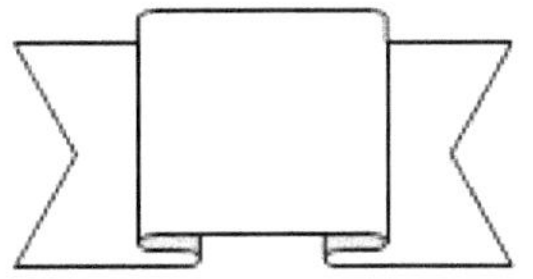

You can spend so much time MISSING someone that you don't realize you may be DISMISSING the next greatest someone in your life!

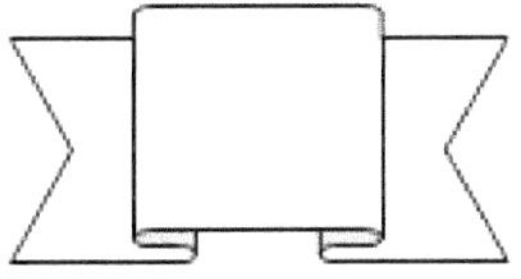

Sometimes letting go means letting grow. For both of you!

There are always three sides to every story. Yours, theirs and the unbiased truth. It doesn't mean anyone is wrong, just seeing it and feeling it differently!

Sometimes the best thing you can do for a friend or loved one is close your mouth and open your ears. They may need someone to listen more than give advice. Learn to be a good listener!

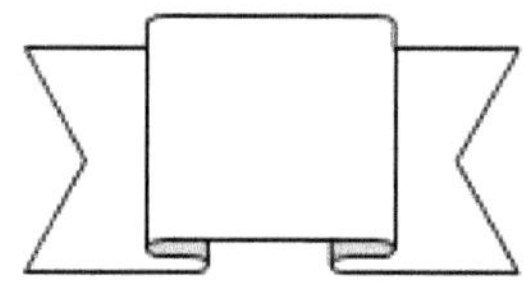

You can open up a Gucci bag and find a fake diamond or open up a paper bag and find a real one. Don't get caught up in the wrapping. It's what's inside that counts. An honest, loving, caring and giving heart is the greatest jewel out there!

Fear, hatred and ignorance can change a LIFE in a moment. Love, understanding and compassion can change the WORLD in that very same moment!

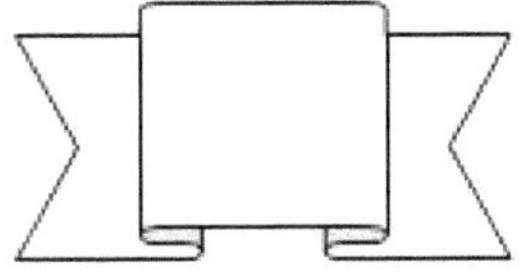

Attitude and Altitude can directly affect each other. You can be flying so high that you crash and burn. Control both your Attitude and Altitude and fly happily forever!

In the span of 24 hours, today becomes yesterday and yesterday remains. The present is just what it says, a PRESENT. Open it with anticipation, use it lovingly and treasure it till it becomes yesterday!

Sponges and tape recorders live among us in the form of children. They absorb and repeat everything we do and say. Don't get angry with a child who does or says something they learned from you. Be the best example you can be!

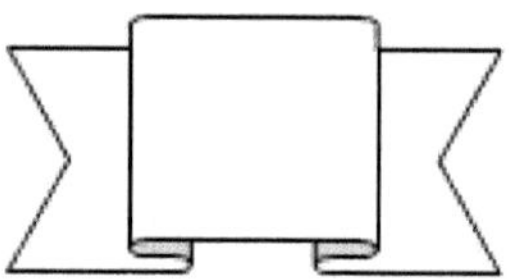

For some the easiest thing is to be hard and the hardest thing to be is easy. Find the balance between the two and find an Angel inside you!

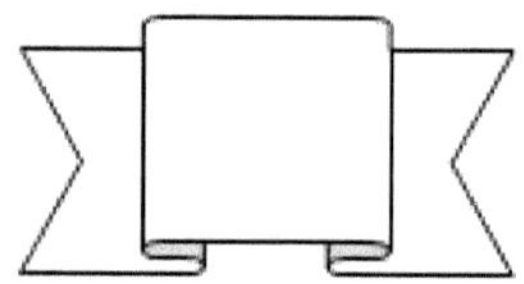

Instead of spending your life searching for the person of your dreams, try finding the person of your soul. When you find them, all your dreams will come true!

After a heartbreak, you can spend your whole life testing the water before going back into the pool of love or you can trust yourself and let the water revive you. Just make sure you've learned how to swim this time!

There is a fine line between Independence and Indifference. If you perceive yourself to be so independent that you don't care if you're alone, don't complain when you find you truly are!

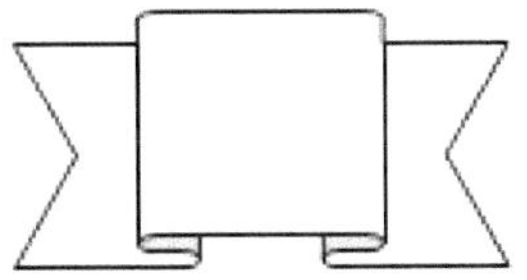

In life and in love, expect little and appreciate everything!

Try not to hold someone so high up on a pedestal. Even the smallest mistake will send them crashing to the ground in your eyes and they will hurt as much as you!

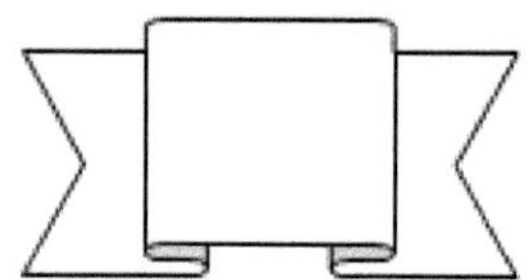

Throughout your life there are going to be people who like you for the things that you do and others who will not for the very same things. Don't try and figure out why, just be yourself!

There is nothing more beautiful than Seeing someone smile. Nothing more gratifying than Making someone smile!

Vision is more than seeing with your eyes. It is also seeing with your heart. Sharing is more than giving something you have. It is also sharing things you dream of, like and cherish!

Sometimes people don't give up on us. They just become weary from trying to break through the walls we've put up. If someone is important to you, break a few walls yourself and meet them in the middle with open arms!

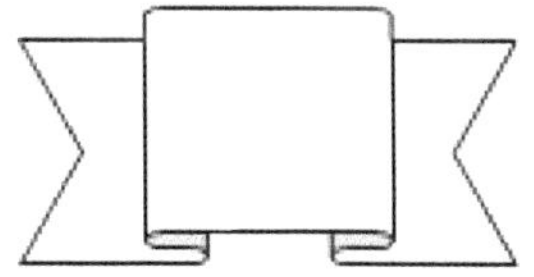

A great leader not only inspires others to have confidence and faith in them but in themselves as well!

Just as a caterpillar must go through the agonizing process of shedding its layers to become a beautiful butterfly, so must we shed our layers of mistrust, anger and hatred to become beautiful!

Boredom and bitterness in life are as dangerous as fire and gasoline. Avoid the deadly explosion by keeping your head, heart and soul busy with good deeds and the bitterness will disappear on its own!

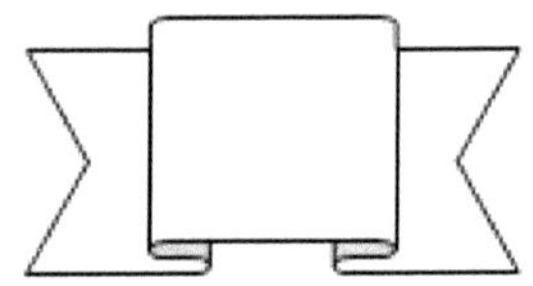

When something is over, no matter how it ended, look forward with anticipation of better things to come and look back with gratitude for the experience and lessons learned. No change is without purpose!

Peace begins with understanding, which begins with explaining, which begins with communicating, which begins with sharing, which begins with giving, which begins with caring, which begins with learning, which begins with living!

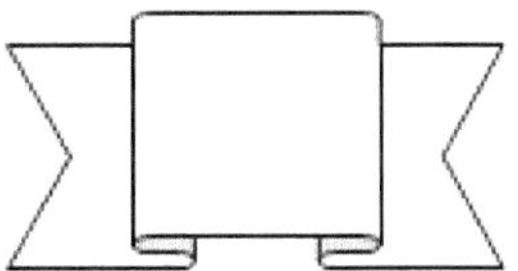

I like you, you're a good person, you have worth, you are loved are all things we need to say to each other and to ourselves every day!

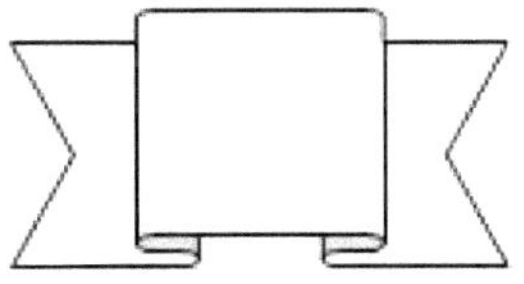

At least once a day try and look at the world with the excitement of a child, the joy of a pet when you come home, the purity of a person of God and the love of a baby! Life can be difficult but we don't have to!

We are sometimes afraid to dream due to painful memories we have locked inside. But we must continue to dream, to remember, to learn, to grow, to forgive and to hope so we can love once again and sleep through the night!

Unselfishness breeds character, character breeds strength, strength breeds direction, direction breeds faith, faith breeds hope and hope breeds love!

From the moment we are born, God gives us a blank book to write our life story in. Each book should be filled with happy memories, good deeds, decency, honor and integrity. God's forgiveness is the eraser!

Don't spend so much time trying to create a character or personality that you forget who you really are!

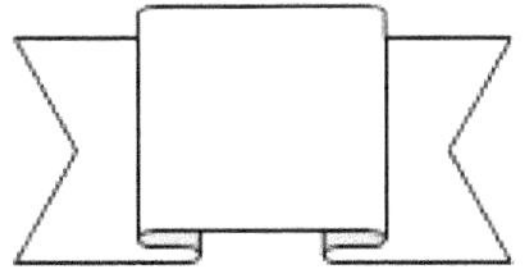

Like our fingerprints, in our hearts and soul we are all special and unique!

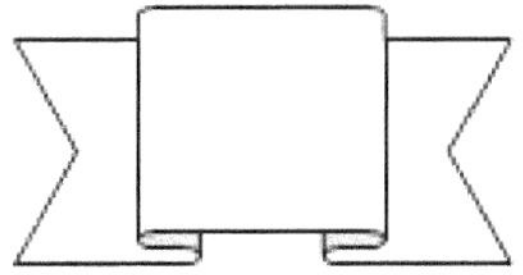

There are no medicines on earth that have the healing powers of a hug or a smile, holding the hand of a child or the love of a pet!

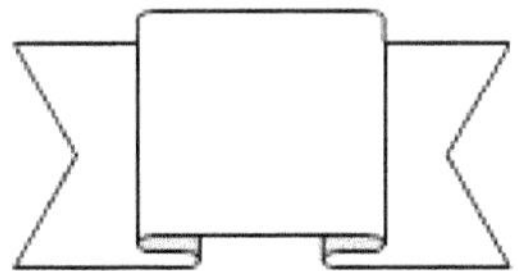

If someone hasn't met your expectations, it is not necessarily their fault. Sometimes our own impatience or even fear destroys the natural growth of a relationship!

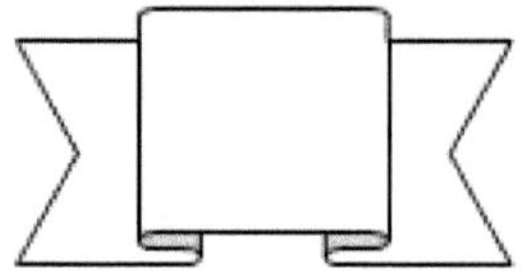

In life and love, the keys to happiness are patience and direction. Place yourself on the right road and have the patience to keep going till you find your destination!

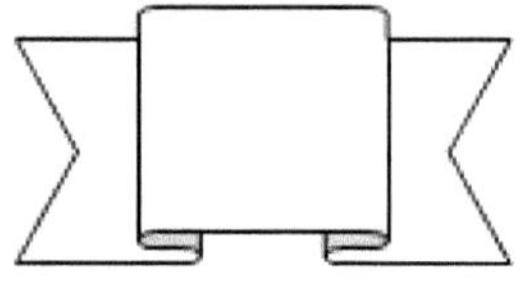

Never grieve in secret. Speak about it, cry about it, shout about it. Balance your heart with sweet memories, love and gratitude for the time you had together!

True love should not be determined by who makes a difference in your life as much who allows "you" to make a difference in "theirs"!

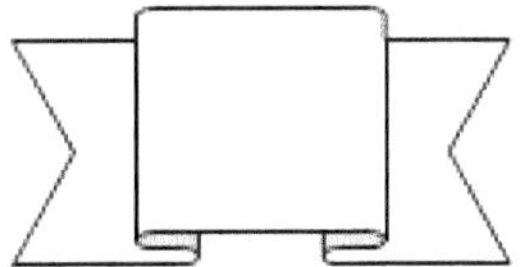

There is contentment in knowing that you are exactly where God wants you to be right now. But never be so content that you forget that there is more for you to do and more lives for you to touch along the way!

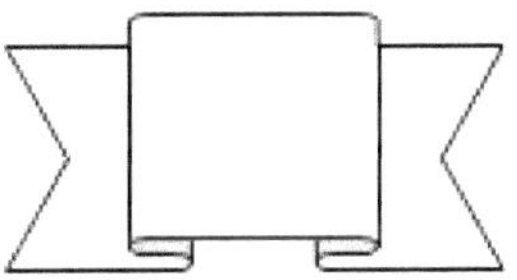

True love never gives false hope, unfulfilled promises or asks another to wait while you decide. Let them go to love another and be happy. Then live with your decision!

Whether or not you believe that Jesus died and rose from the dead for us, believe in the concept of reward for sacrifice, the inner peace of being unselfish and the joy of unconditional love!

If you allow others to make fun of a friend, secretly smile when they fall, and envy their achievements, THEY are not a friend and worse than that YOU are not a friend!

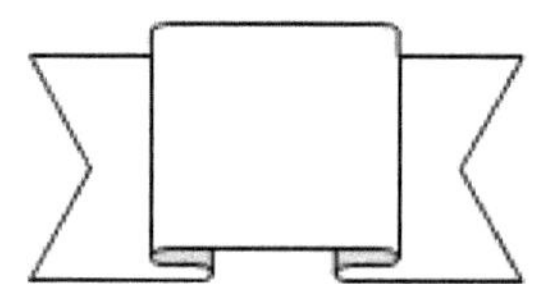

There are those who look at Faith and Belief in the same manner they look at the ocean. They see it end at the horizon. Yet others see the horizon and KNOW that there are greater things beyond our sight!

Love is one of God's fruit. It is sweet and always in season. But it always needs nurturing to keep it alive and growing!

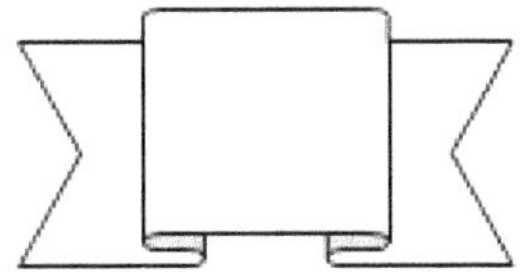

No matter how hard we try, if someone's heart and mind is closed, they will not see or hear us.

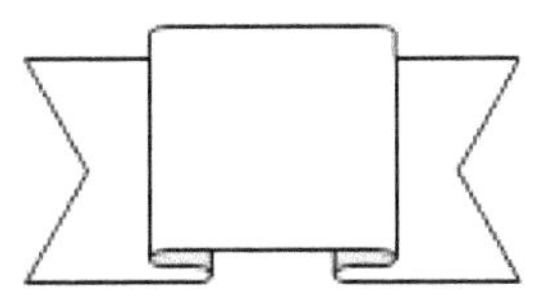

Tears are often our hearts quietly saying the things pride and anger won't allow our mouths to say out loud!

Imitation may be the sincerest form of flattery. But it only flatters the one being imitated. There is only one YOU in this world. Don't deprive the world of YOU. Like yourself, trust yourself for that's who you spend 100% of your time with!

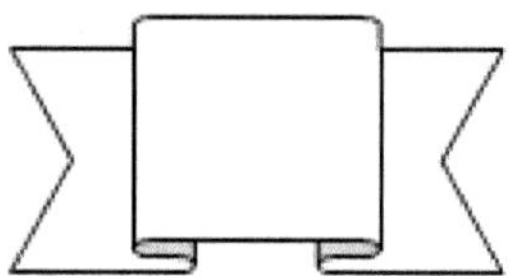

In the end we will remember the laughs more than the tears, successes more than failures, love more than heartache, smiles more than tears. Build happy, loving and positive memories for everyone who comes into your life!

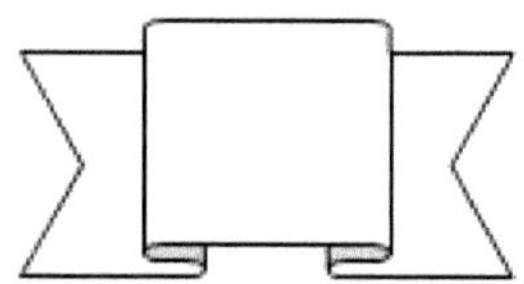

At this very moment, there is someone praying for your happiness, your health and your prosperity. Return the favor every day!

Even the most brilliant flame needs air and space to keep burning brightly or it will smother and die. The same holds true for our relationships. Fuel the fire when needed, but give it some space to live!

You may convince yourself that something is too good to be true. The truth just may be that you are getting a preview of what could be. Don't let mistrust, fear or insecurity make you throw away something wonderful!

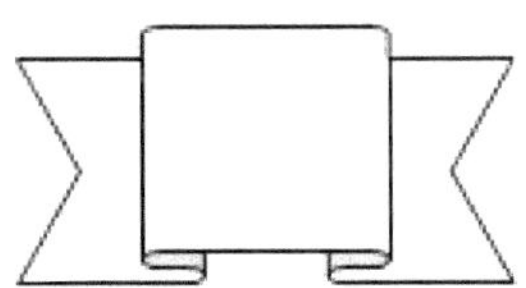

Sometimes someone new in our life can bring up a memory you were trying to forget and we push them away. Never let mistakes from the past destroy another's promise for the future!

The word "conviction" is more than a legal term. It is a way of thinking and living, a path to inner peace, strength and growth. We must live by our own convictions. Respect yourself and others will too!

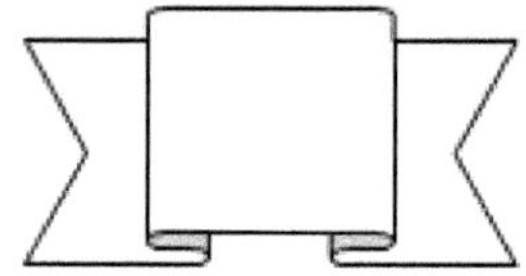

Aspirin can heal a headache. A bandaid can heal a scrape. Stitches can heal a wound. But there is no medicine to heal a reputation scarred by rumors and gossip. Watch your tongue!

You can "say" you love someone. You can "say" you're there for someone. You can "say" you need someone. You can "say" you respect someone. Starting today let's all "show" more and "say" less! Whadd'ya SAY?

Be a good person, be a caring person and those who can't or won't see it, never will!

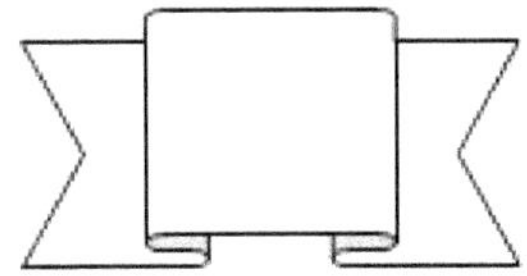

That idiot weaving in and out of traffic may be rushing to a loved one in trouble. That idiot fumbling with the money and taking too much time at the checkout may have trouble seeing. That idiot talking too loud in the movie theater may be almost deaf. We never really know what is happening in someone's life, so let's try and smile more and grunt less!

Sometimes trying to be successful can completely take over your sense of sight. Just as someone is receiving an award, they remember all the people who helped them on the project but forget the people who were there during the struggles, disappointments and tough times! These are the people who should matter most. The ones who believed in you before you were recognized!

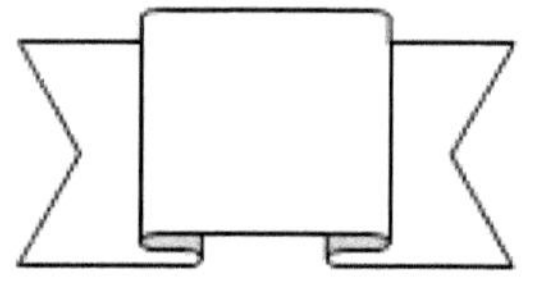

In any relationship, love, business, (friends or family), your treatment of others will determine your path to success. Look at the big picture. If you grow just as big as the picture grows, you may need to rethink the path you put yourself on. Success, happiness and love cannot be achieved or enjoyed alone!

Trust is one of the most important words in any relationship. You must trust yourself to allow yourself to trust someone else!

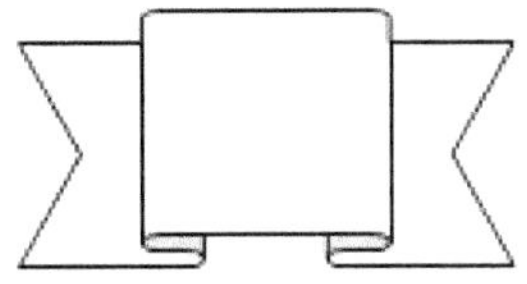

Today we celebrate Freedom. Let's take it a step further. Free yourself of hatred. Free yourself from abuse. Free yourself from bad memories. Free yourself to be happy. Free yourself from anger. Smile at someone today, it's Free!

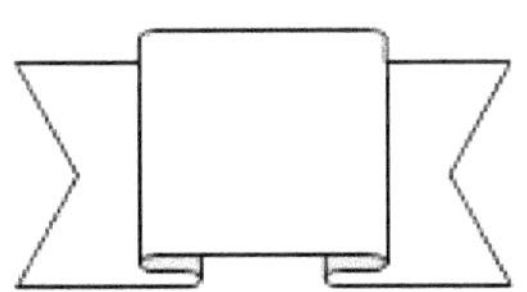

You can EXPECT people to do what you want and be disappointed or ACCEPT things as they happen and be happy. Two simple words that sound the same but have two completely different meanings!

There is nothing more beautiful than to see someone's smile. Let's start a United Beautification Program today in our daily lives. Get as many people as you can to smile. If they're short, give them one of yours. If you're short, borrow one of theirs! Ready, set, GOOOOOO!

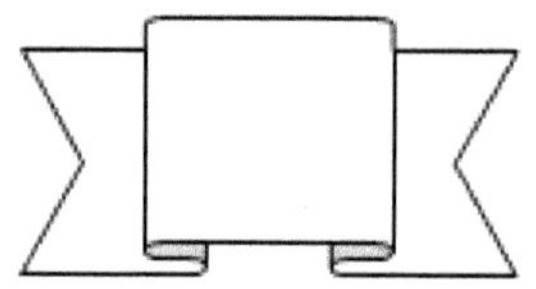

With the right person, you don't need heels to stand tall. You don't need muscles show strength. You don't need lingerie to be sexy. You don't need to tell jokes to make them smile. Be YOU! If they don't see YOU, keep looking!

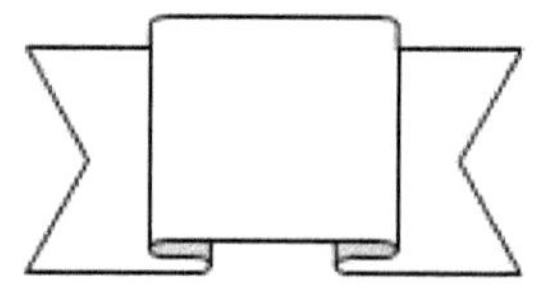

If you don't ask somoene to stay, don't be upset when they leave!

Sometimes when we let someone go free, we may be subconsciously letting ourselves go free instead! Either way, it's not an easy task.

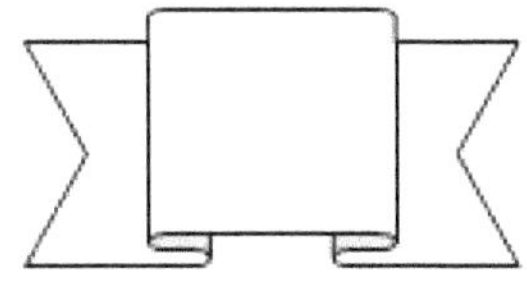

In any relationship, (business, love, family or friends), if ANY part of that relationship has to be kept a secret, something is very wrong!

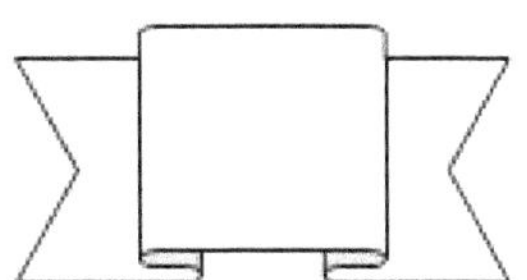

If the same problems keep occurring in relationship after relationship, you can take the easy way out and say "I keep falling for the same person". When actually you just may be making the same mistakes and the biggest mistake of all is that the right one may have slipped away!

Absence sometimes makes the heart grow fonder but Abstinence sometimes makes it wander!

Too often people blame God for unpleasant events and praise each other for good ones. Let's try reversing that way of thinking! You can't spell GOOD without GOD!

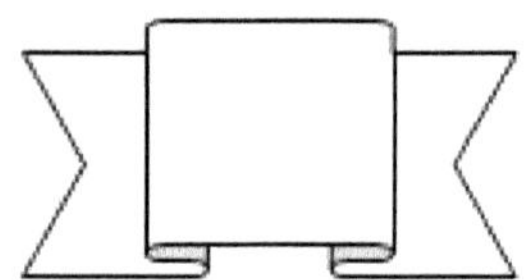

Sometimes we can get so blinded by our own self-inflicted tears that we fail to see the tears were are inflicting on those who care about us! We must learn to open our eyes, heart and mind to the world around us!

The secret to stability in any relationship is like standing in the ocean at the shore. If you plant your feet firmly in the sand and only look forward, you will be knocked down. But if you remain flexible and keep your eyes open, you will see that big wave coming long before it reaches you!

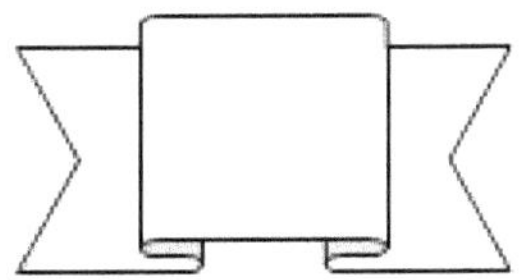

Never get so angry or vengeful that you feel the need to teach someone a lesson. Thirst for revenge never quenches the bitterness and the lesson is never learned! Take a breath, turn to God and live your life free from anger!

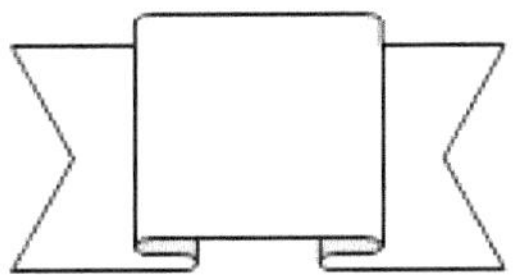

Change can be a scary thing. But staying where you are and being unhappy should be even scarier!

Those three little words "I Love You" are important to say in a relationship. But so are "I need you", "I like you", "I respect you", "I was wrong", "please forgive me", "let's try again", and "don't leave me"! Nothing is understood until it's been said!

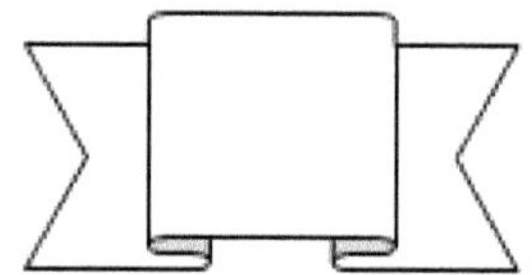

If you live your life playing the victim and blaming everyone else for your mistakes, you might as well remove all the mirrors from your house. None of us is perfect. Some try to be and some just never try!

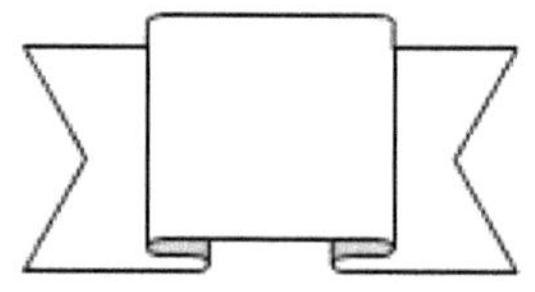

If your dreams have someone special in them, tell them about it. They might be having the same dreams!

People can say things to try and hurt you and attack your character. But they can only do damage if you let them. Never defend yourself to a person who's opinion of you doesn't matter! Stand tall, smile in their face and walk away whistling!

Excuses are the camouflage in the war between honesty and deceit. It's always better to tell the truth and have to dance, than to be caught in a lie and face the music!

Don't ask someone to wait while you try to get out of a bad relationship. Get out of the relationship first and then ask them to hold your hand through the transition and beyond. If they're still available!

Don't spend so much time holding on to someone from "yesterday" that you miss the chance to hold someone special "today and "tomorrow"!

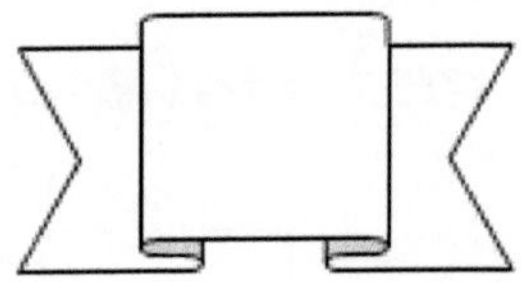

Peace in your life begins with understanding, which begins with explaining, which begins with talking, which begins with sharing, which begins with giving, which begins with caring, which begins with learning, which begins with living!

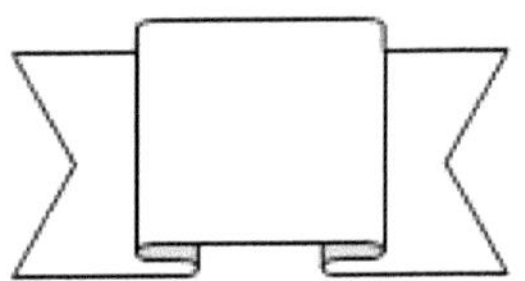

Be aware of the people who come in and out of your life only when it benefits them. Surround yourself with people who come into your life when it benefits YOU too!

The biggest lie anyone can tell you or you can tell yourself is claiming to not know what's right or wrong! When that point is reached, the struggle between doing what's "right" and doing what you "want" begins. Always try to do what's right for the sake of everyone involved!

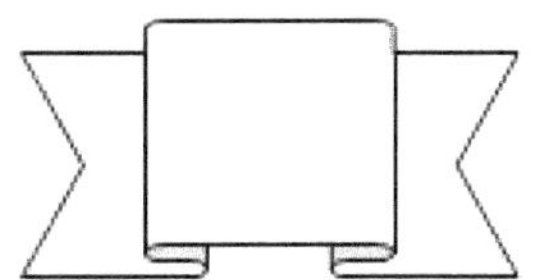

In the workplace and in life, if you constantly look for the shortcut or easy way out of things, you will most certainly find yourself cut short and easily out the door with nobody to blame but yourself. Whatever job you have, be the best one there ever was or ever will be!

If you do things for people expecting a thank you, you have defeated the purpose of your act and created a wedge between you and that person. Do good for the pure sake of goodness!

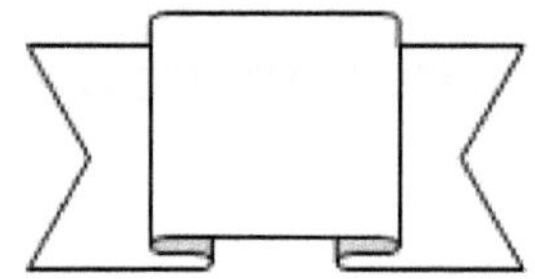

Don't beat yourself up for mistakes made or errors. They are God's way of pointing out what you need to work on. We are all born not knowing "anything" and will pass not knowing "everything". The key is to be the best human we can be in between!

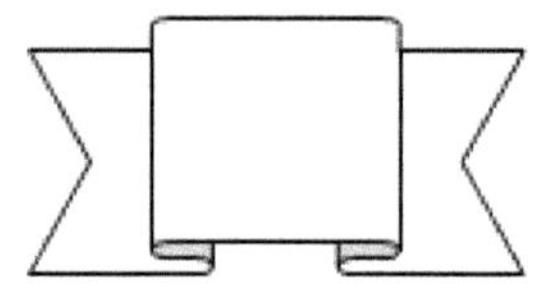

More important than the "heat" of passion is the "warmth" of companionship!

Don't let your fear of heartache or disappointment stop you from believing in a happy ending. It may not be the ending you dreamed of but just may be even happier than you dreamed!

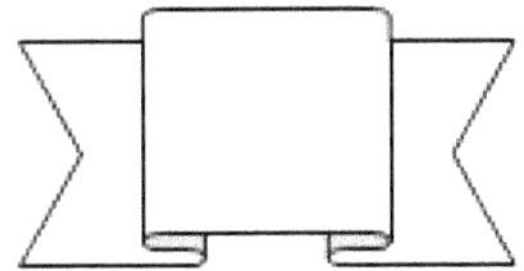

Guardian Angels do not just live "among" us, they live "within" us. Each of us has the ability to be one, don't pass up the opportunity when it's your turn. Shine up those halos folks. We're all we have!!

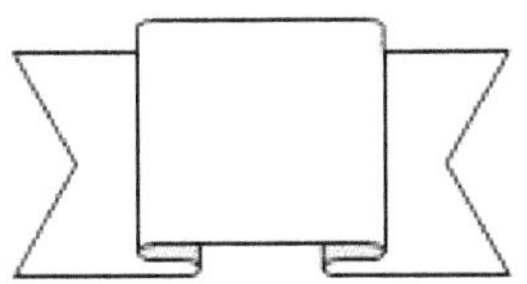

We are never so "close" to peace as when we are "open" to change!

Just as you cannot enjoy fruit from a tree until you have patiently allowed it to grow naturally. You can never experience true love until you let it grow naturally. Feed it with love, care and compassion, then you both will enjoy the fruits of your efforts!

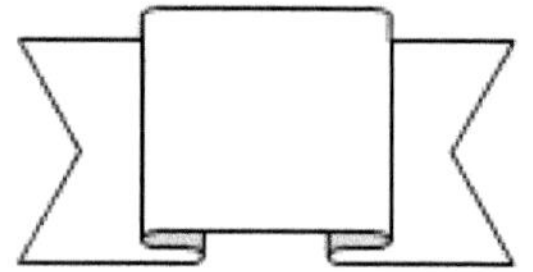

We can spend so much time and energy dwelling on our tomorrows and yesterdays, that today gets neglected. In the span of 24 hours, today becomes yesterday, tomorrow becomes today.

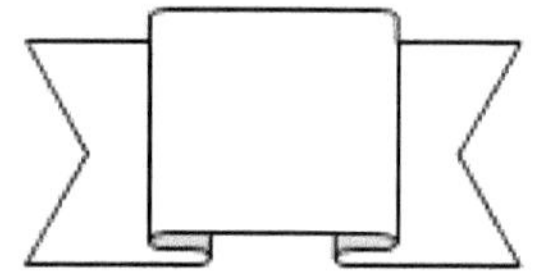

Mistakes in life are merely lessons of life and should not be dwelled on. The true mistakes in life are when we repeat the ones that hurt us! Live and Learn, it's that simple!

When a child reaches out their arms everyone immediately understands that they want to be picked up, hugged and held. Sometimes the same request from an adult isn't as obvious, but the need is the same. Look for the signals in their eyes, sighs and cries! A hug costs nothing but it's worth a million!

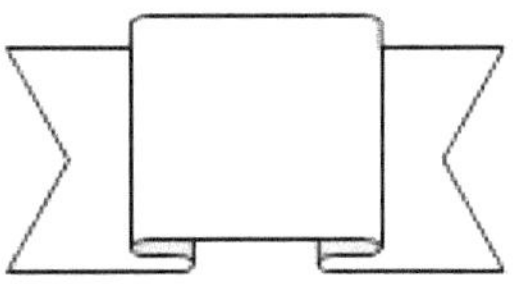

Sometimes it just takes some time!

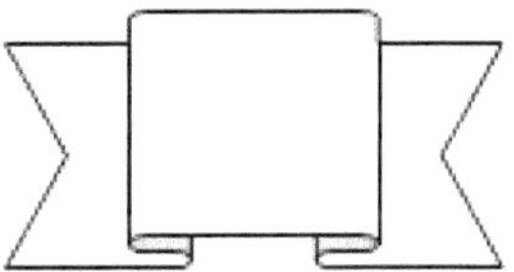

A ripple in the water can go on endlessly. A splash is a one time event. In life and love, be a ripple that calmly moves and motivates rather than a big splash that draws attention and disrupts the calmness!

True love and true friendship transcend time and distance. When it's pure, real and unconditional, time or distance apart never matters.

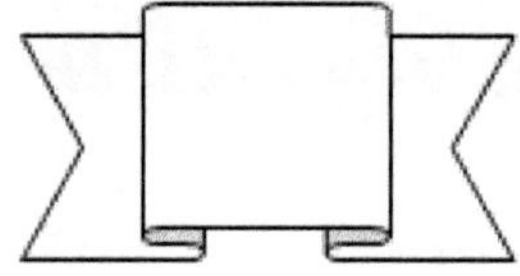

You can build a "House" to make one dream come true or you can build a "Home" and make all your dreams come true!

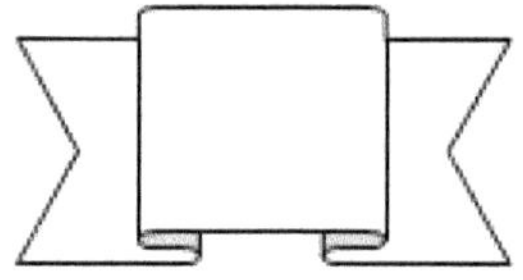

You can turn the other cheek so many times that your neck looks like a pretzel. Sometimes you have to "stand up" and "speak up" rather than "shut up" and "put up" with disrespect. Take your lumps when you deserve them but give them back when someone else deserves theirs!

Sunday is the Lord's day. He gave us this day to rest and reflect. Let's make Sunday the day we call relatives or friends, visit cemeteries, have a family picnic, sit and talk to our chikdren or visit someone in the hospital. Make every Sunday a meaningful day for someone in your life!

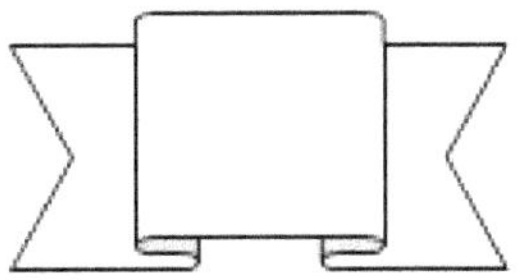

Some people use "I'm sorry" like it's an eraser on a blackboard thinking it wipes the slate clean. Instead, take each item on that blackboard and apologize for each hurt one at a time, mean it and try your best not to repeat any of them!

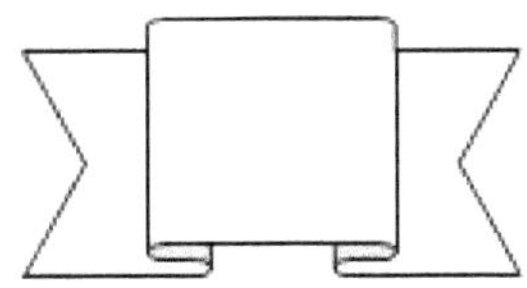

Don't measure yourself based on someone else's achievements or acquisitions. The true measure of "you" is based on the generosity of your heart, the compassion of your mind and the kindness of your soul!

If we never "own" up to our responsibilities, we may find out that we are left on our "own" down the road!

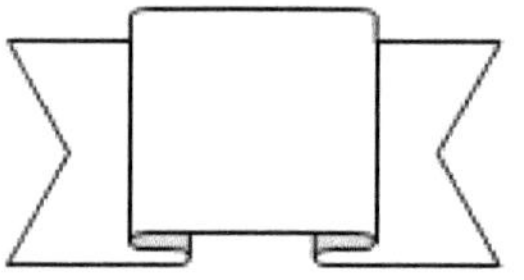

The best way to get rid of the darkness is to shed light on it! Nobody should suffer in silence. Be someone else's light every chance you get. Even if they seem to wanna stay in the dark

For some the easiest thing in the world is to be hard and the hardest thing is to be easy. Find a balance between the two and you will find balance in your life!

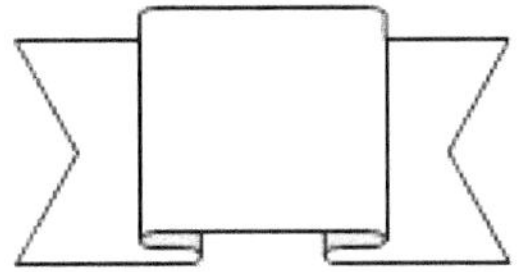

If you think that someone doesn't say I love you enough, listen for it with your eyes instead. They just might be saying it every day through their actions!

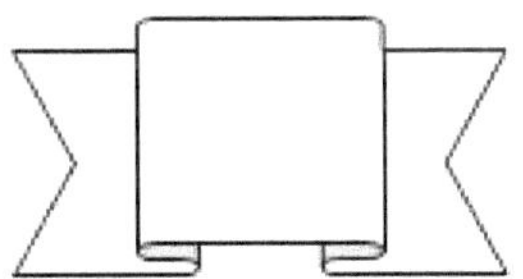

Living under expectations of failure, anyone will fail. They key is to look passed the imperfections and work from there! That is if you truly want everyone to succeed!

You can spend your whole life testing the water before going back into the pool of life and love OR you can trust your instincts and let the water refresh and revive you. Just make sure you've learned how to swim this time

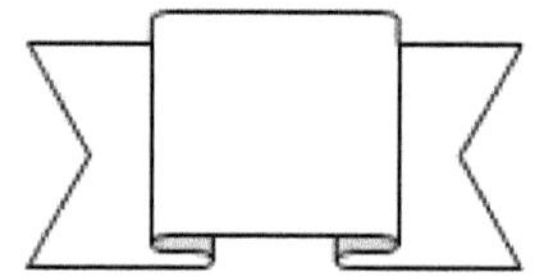

We may not find comfort knowing that others are going through similiar financial, physical and/or emotional issues. But we must always find compassion for them!

Communication is more than speaking. It's expressing your feelings, hopes, fears, dreams. It's realizing that someone needs to hear these things as much as you need to say them

You can be whoever you want to be and be happy. But you'll never be happy being whoever someone else wants you to be!

The pain of letting someone go can be unbearable at times. But that pain merely signifies the love you have for them. Be happy for that pain knowing the bond will never be broken!

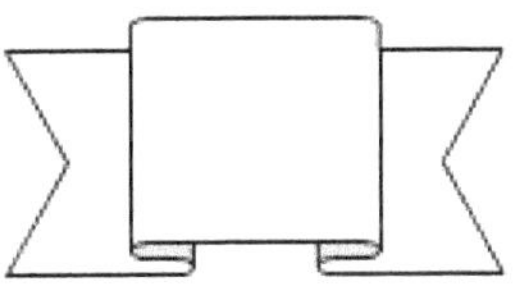

Sometimes are told how we should act and react. We are told to play it cool, take the initiative, don't push, be the agressor, be shy, be bold! But when it's right, the "easiest" thing to do is be yourself and be loved for it!

If you think that you "can't" or that you "can", you're right either way! Always think you can!

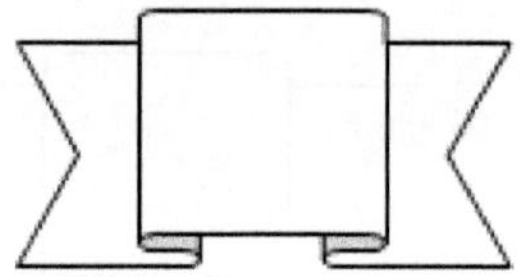

One of the "easiest" things to do is form an opinion about someone! One of the "hardest" things to do is admit that you were wrong!

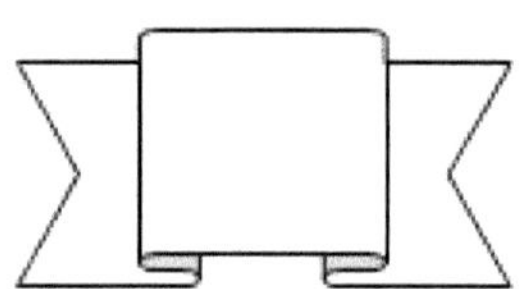

Nobody knows what a person is really like inside except them and God. If you really want to know someone, put all ASSumptions aside and look into their soul. You may be pleasantly surprised!

For some people, the road to success is so long, they are too tired to enjoy it. For others, the road is so short they get too tired trying to maintain it and never enjoy it.

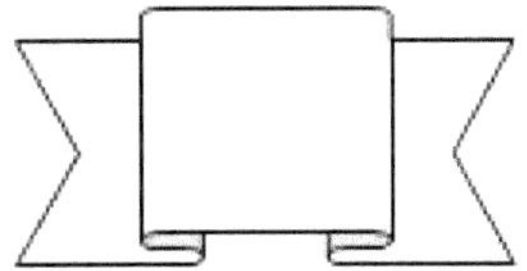

To enjoy the sun, you have to have lived in the rain.
To enjoy the rain, you have to have lived in the sun.
To enjoy love, you have to have a broekn heart!

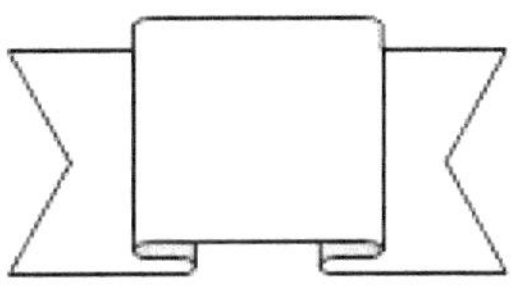

It may seem like someone has stopped trying to communicate and break down your walls. It doesn't mean they stopped caring. They just stepped back hoping and praying that one day you'll try just as hard!

Tell someone "I Love You" for the way they make you feel about THEM, as well as the way they make you feel about YOURSELF!

In any relationship, be it friendship, family or love, try not to hold someone so high on a pedestal. Even the smallest mistake will send them crashing to the floor and the fall will hurt them as much as you!

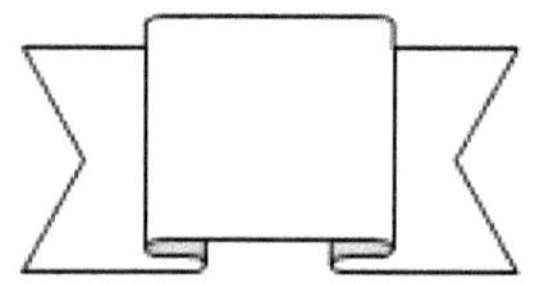

Boredom and bitterness are as dangerous as fire and gasoline. Avoid the deadly explosion by keeping your heart and soul busy with good deeds and the bitterness will disappear on its own!

Change can be a scary thing. But staying where you are and being unhappy should be even scarier! Trust your instincts, trust your heart and trust God!

If you find yourself becoming lost on Life's Highway, turn on your GPS.

(God Provides Strength)!

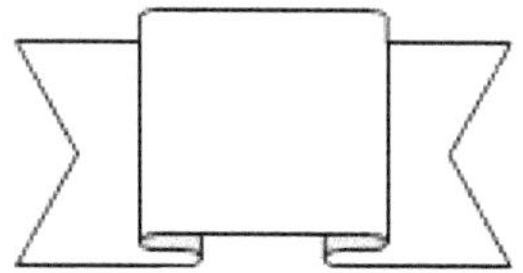

Just as a caterpillar must go through the process of shedding it's skin before becoming a beautiful butterfly, so must we go through the process of shedding the skins of mistrust, disrespect and anger before we can become a beautiful human. Start shedding yours today!

A true friend not only hears your cries but feels your pain and understands!

The human brain understands that sometimes there is no answer. The human heart sometimes does not. Belief and faith are the referees in this never ending battle.

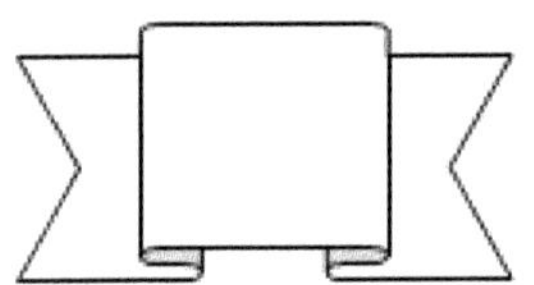

Telling someone "You owe me big time" after a favor, demeans the act of kindness, demeans the person receiving the favor and demeans you. If someone needs a favor, do it with no expectations, no speeches and no payback required. Give to give, not give to get!

Heaven's Phone

I still can't believe it, you're really not here, weeks blend into months and months into years. You promised you'd stay, I know how you tried, but God needed you more so I stepped aside. I didn't collapse, did not fall apart, but deep down inside there's a hole in my heart

It comes out of nowhere, a smell or a sound, that's when it hits me that you're not around. So much to remember, so much to forget, you left me too soon is my only regret. My heart breaks a little when I think of when, we planned on tomorrows that would never end.

I try to fight it and hold back the tears, never give in to the grief and the fears. But when those times come and I need to talk, to just hear your voice or go for a walk. We don't need no wires, don't need a dial tone, you always answer when I use Heaven's phone!

Yeah, I try to fight it and hold back the tears, never give in to the grief and the fears. But when those times come and I need to talk, to just hear your voice or go for a walk. We don't need no wires, don't need a dial tone, you always answer when I use Heaven's phone!

Yes you always answer when I use Heaven's phone

You always answer when I use Heaven's phone

www.ingramcontent.com/pod-product-compliance
Ingram Content Group UK Ltd.
Pitfield, Milton Keynes, MK11 3LW, UK
UKHW051136260726
13967UKWH00010B/3081